KID CHEMISTRY LAB

EXAMINING MIXTURES
& SOLUTIONS

Jessica Rusick

Checkerboard
Library

An Imprint of Abdo Publishing
abdobooks.com

ABDOBOOKS.COM

Published by Abdo Publishing, a division of ABDO, PO Box 398166, Minneapolis, Minnesota 55439. Copyright © 2023 by Abdo Consulting Group, Inc. International copyrights reserved in all countries. No part of this book may be reproduced in any form without written permission from the publisher. Checkerboard Library™ is a trademark and logo of Abdo Publishing.

Printed in the United States of America, North Mankato, Minnesota
052022
092022

THIS BOOK CONTAINS RECYCLED MATERIALS

Design and Production: Kelly Doudna, Mighty Media, Inc.
Editor: Liz Salzmann
Cover Photograph: Lekyum/iStockphoto
Interior Photographs: adriaticfoto/Shutterstock Images, p. 7; Ahanov Michael/Shutterstock Images, p. 21; fotozick/Shutterstock Images, p. 9; Mighty Media, Inc., pp. 26, 27, 28, 29; Natalia Saudi/Shutterstock Images, p. 15; New Africa/Shutterstock Images, p. 17; OlgaKhorkova/Shutterstock Images, p. 11; Pavel L Photo and Video/Shutterstock Images, p. 19; Peter Bocklandt/Shutterstock Images, pp. 12–13; Pollyana Ventura/iStockphoto, p. 25; Sea Wave/Shutterstock Images, p. 8; Sergey Novikov/Shutterstock Images, p. 5; udaix/Shutterstock Images, p. 23

Library of Congress Control Number: 2021970088

Publisher's Cataloging-in-Publication Data
Names: Rusick, Jessica, author.
Title: Examining mixtures & solutions / by Jessica Rusick.
Description: Minneapolis, Minnesota : Abdo Publishing, 2023 | Series: Kid chemistry lab | Includes online resources and index.
Identifiers: ISBN 9781532198991 (lib. bdg.) | ISBN 9781098272920 (ebook)
Subjects: LCSH: Chemistry--Juvenile literature. | Mixtures--Juvenile literature. | Solution (Chemistry)--Juvenile literature. | Science projects--Juvenile literature.
Classification: DDC 540--dc23

CONTENTS

What Are Mixtures & Solutions? 4

Heterogeneous or Homogeneous? 6

Solutions 10

Suspensions & Colloids 14

Solubility, Saturation & Concentration . . 16

Separating Mixtures 20

Mixtures in Everyday Life 24

Marker Chromatography 26

Baking Soda Crystals 28

Glossary 30

Online Resources 31

Index 32

WHAT ARE MIXTURES & SOLUTIONS?

A mixture is a combination of two or more substances. We encounter mixtures every day. They can be made of solids, gases, or liquids. Pouring milk into cereal makes a milk and cereal mixture. Salad is a mixture of different ingredients. Even air is a mixture of different gases!

A solution is a type of mixture. In a solution, one substance is **dissolved** in another. Stirring salt into water, for example, makes a saltwater solution. In some mixtures, you can easily see the different parts. But you can't see all the parts in a solution. A saltwater solution looks like regular water. You can't see the salt that is dissolved in it.

The water in the ocean is a saltwater solution.

Chapter 2
HETEROGENEOUS OR HOMOGENEOUS?

Mixtures are either **heterogeneous** or **homogeneous**. Homogeneous mixtures are the same throughout. Mixing sugar in water creates a homogeneous mixture. The **dissolved** sugar spreads out evenly through the water. If you sampled different parts of the mixture, they would all contain the same amount of sugar.

A heterogeneous mixture is not the same throughout. Different parts of the mixture have different substances. A chocolate chip cookie is a heterogeneous mixture. If you took samples of the cookie, the samples would be different from each other. Some samples would have chocolate chips. Others wouldn't.

One method scientists use to tell whether a mixture is homogeneous is viewing it with a microscope.

Sometimes it's possible to see whether a mixture is **heterogeneous** or **homogeneous**. A chocolate chip cookie is clearly not the same throughout. So, it is heterogeneous. Homogeneous mixtures like sugar water look the same everywhere. You cannot see the different parts.

Some heterogeneous mixtures look homogeneous. A patch of soil may appear to be uniform. But soil is a heterogeneous mixture. Each soil sample will contain different amounts of rocks, minerals, and other substances.

Cream looks homogeneous to the naked eye.

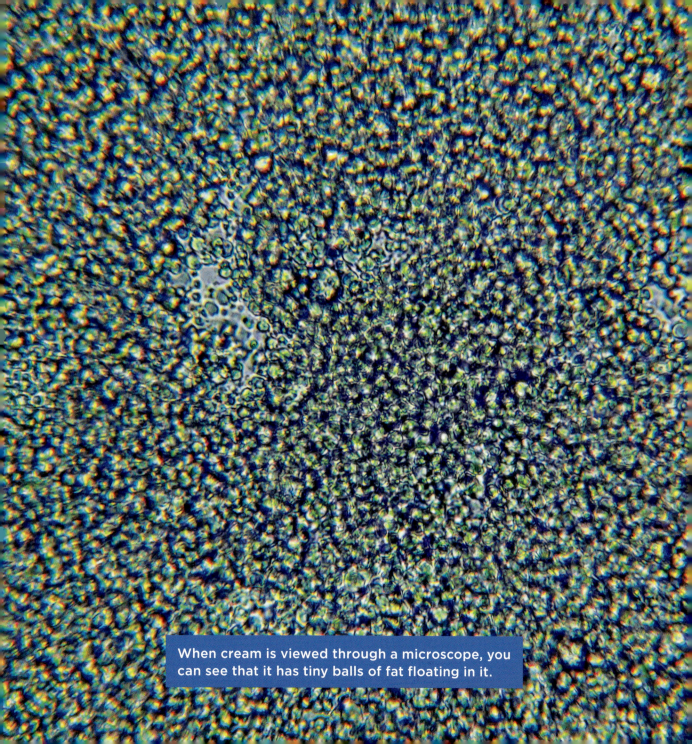

When cream is viewed through a microscope, you can see that it has tiny balls of fat floating in it.

Chapter 3

SOLUTIONS

A solution is a **homogeneous** mixture. It is made of a **solute** and a **solvent**. When mixed, the solute **dissolves** and becomes part of the solvent. So, the solute is the substance being dissolved. The solvent is the substance dissolving the solute. In a saltwater solution, salt is the solute. Water is the solvent.

Many solvents are liquids. But they can be solids or gases as well. Solutes can also be solids, liquids, or gases. A solution made with at least one metal is called an **alloy**. Brass is an alloy. It is made of zinc dissolved in copper.

Air is a solution. Its solvent is nitrogen. The main solute is oxygen, but air also contains small amounts of other gases. ▶

Two liquids can also form a solution. Vinegar contains a liquid **solute** in a liquid **solvent**. The solute is **acetic acid**. The solvent is water. The ability of two liquids to form a solution is called miscibility. Acetic acid and water are miscible because they mix to form a solution. Oil and water are immiscible. If you try to mix them, the substances separate into different layers.

Water is often the solvent in a liquid solution. It can dissolve more substances than any other liquid!

Chapter 4
SUSPENSIONS & COLLOIDS

Suspensions and colloids are types of mixtures that have larger solute particles. A suspension has large particles that are large enough to see. Mixing sand and water creates a suspension. When stirred, the sand seems to mix with the water. But the sand does not **dissolve**. Eventually, it will settle to the bottom of the container.

A colloid has medium-sized solute particles. They are bigger than those in a solution and smaller than those in a suspension. The particles are large enough to see. But they are small enough that they don't settle out of the **solvent**. Smoke is a colloid. It contains medium-sized **soot** particles mixed with gases.

Hot cocoa is a suspension. Most of the powder stays mixed into the milk. But some will stick to the side and bottom of the cup.

Chapter 5
SOLUBILITY, SATURATION & CONCENTRATION

Solutes have different solubilities. This is the amount of solute that will **dissolve** in a given amount of **solvent**. When no more solute can be dissolved in a solution, the solution is saturated. Any more added solute will settle to the bottom. An unsaturated solvent can dissolve more solute.

For example, salt is soluble in water. About 1.27 ounces (36 g) of salt can dissolve in 0.42 cups (100 mL) of water that is 68 degrees Fahrenheit (20°C). The solution is then saturated.

Stirring can make solutes dissolve faster. But it doesn't affect how much solute dissolves.

A **solvent's** temperature affects the amount of **solute** that **dissolves**. Generally, hotter solvents can dissolve more solute. So, if the water is heated to 140 degrees Fahrenheit (60°C), about 1.3 ounces (37 g) of salt can dissolve in it before it becomes saturated.

Pressure can increase saturation. **Carbonated** drinks have **carbon dioxide** gas dissolved in them. The pressure of the bottle or can causes the water to dissolve more carbon dioxide than it normally could. This is called supersaturation.

A solution's concentration is how much solute it contains. A solution with more solute is more concentrated than one with less solute. Scientists use different methods to determine how concentrated a solution is. One method is to measure the number of grams of solute per liter of solvent.

After a bottle or can of soda is opened, the carbon dioxide in the water starts escaping. Eventually, the soda becomes flat because all the carbon dioxide has escaped.

Chapter 6
SEPARATING MIXTURES

Sometimes, combining two substances produces a chemical reaction. A chemical reaction transforms substances into other substances. Mixtures do not produce chemical reactions. If sugar and water are mixed, they do not react. The water is still water. The sugar is still sugar, even though it is **dissolved**. No substances have been changed into other substances.

After a chemical reaction, it is often impossible to change new substances back into old substances. But mixtures can be separated back into their original parts. Some mixtures can be separated by hand.

A kitchen strainer is a type of filter. It separates a mixture of water and solid food.

Other mixtures, such as suspensions, can be separated with a filter. The filter catches large solid particles. It lets smaller liquid particles through. Sand and water can be separated this way. The filter catches sand, but not the water.

Solutions cannot be separated by a filter. That's because the **solute** particles are too small. One way to separate a liquid solution is by **distillation**. This involves heating and then cooling the solution.

Mixtures can also be separated by chromatography. In this method, some of the mixture is placed on a solid, such as paper. A liquid or gas then flows through the solid, carrying the mixture with it. Heavier parts of the mixture are carried shorter distances. Lighter parts are carried longer distances. This separates the mixture into different layers.

DISTILLATION

Distillation is often used to separate a solution that is made of substances that have different **boiling points**. The solution is put in a distilling **flask**. The flask is heated until the substance with the lower boiling point boils. It turns into vapor. The vapor rises into a tube called a **condenser**. There, the vapor is cooled until it becomes liquid again. The condenser moves the liquid to a receiving flask. The substance with the higher boiling point remains in the distilling flask.

DISTILLATION APPARATUS

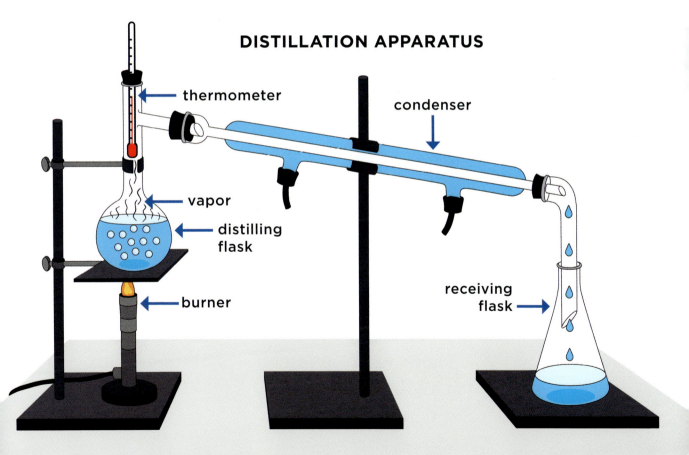

Chapter 7
MIXTURES IN EVERYDAY LIFE

Almost everything we use daily is a mixture. Mixtures are also important to the study of chemistry. Many chemists create, study, and separate mixtures as part of their jobs. Chemists also **analyze** substances to determine what they're made of. They use methods such as chromatography to test the quality of foods and medicines.

Chemists use mixtures to make **varieties** of substances, such as shades of paint. Mixtures also play an important role in improving building materials, such as concrete and metals. They are also used to develop new materials and products. Who knows what interesting new mixtures will be created in the future?

Many arts and crafts supplies, such as paint, are mixtures.

MARKER CHROMATOGRAPHY

WHAT HAPPENS

Black marker ink contains a mixture of different dyes. The dyes can be separated into different layers using chromatography. Each dye contains chemicals of different weights. Lightweight dyes are carried farther up the filter paper by the water. Heavy dyes are carried shorter distances.

EXPERIMENT!

Repeat the project using other colors of nonpermanent marker. Which color separates into the most layers?

MATERIALS

- nonpermanent black marker
- coffee filter
- clear cup
- ruler
- water

STEPS

1 Use a nonpermanent black marker to draw a thick circle in the center of a coffee filter.

2 Fold the coffee filter to form a cone.

3 Fill a cup with about ½ inch (1.25 cm) of water.

4 Place the tip of the filter cone in the water. Be sure the marker line does not touch the water. Fan out the top of the cone so it rests against the rim of the glass.

5 Watch the marker line as water flows up the coffee filter.

THE SCIENTIFIC METHOD

Want to experiment like a real chemist? Follow the scientific method! The scientific method is a process scientists use to answer questions.

1. Ask a question. Research your question to learn more about it.
2. Develop a **hypothesis**. This is your best guess about the answer to your question.
3. Experiment to test your hypothesis. Record what happens during the experiment.
4. Review the results of your experiment to draw a conclusion. Was your hypothesis supported? Why or why not? Share your results with others.

BAKING SODA CRYSTALS

WHAT HAPPENS

The baking soda and water mixture is a saturated solution. The string soaks up the solution. Over a few days, the water **evaporates**, turning into vapor. The baking soda is left behind in the form of crystals.

MATERIALS

- plate
- two jars or glasses
- hot water
- baking soda
- tablespoon
- food coloring
- string
- paper clips

STEPS

1 Place the plate between the two jars. Fill the jars with hot water.

2 Stir baking soda into each jar, one tablespoon at a time. Keep adding baking soda until no more will **dissolve**.

3 Stir a few drops of food coloring into each jar.

4 Tie a paper clip to each end of a piece of string. Place one paper clip in each jar. Let the string hang in a U shape over the plate between the jars. Do not let it touch the plate.

5 Observe the string over the next few days. Be sure not to move the string or the jars. What do you notice?

EXPERIMENT!

Try the project again using sugar or salt instead of baking soda. Which **solute** grows the most crystals? Or, try using different types of string or yarn. How does this affect crystal growth?

GLOSSARY

acetic acid—a colorless liquid that has a strong scent and is the main acid in vinegar.

alloy—a metal made by melting two or more metals, or a metal and another material, and mixing them together.

analyze—to examine something to find out what it is or what makes it work.

boiling point—the temperature at which a substance boils.

carbon dioxide—a heavy, colorless gas that is released when people and animals breathe out and produced when some fuels are burned.

carbonated—combined or infused with carbon dioxide.

condenser—a device used to change a gas into a liquid.

dissolve—to pass into a solution or become liquid.

distill—to separate substances in a mixture by heating and cooling it. The act of distilling is distillation.

evaporate—to change from a liquid or a solid into a vapor.

flask—a type of glass bottle used in scientific laboratories.

heterogeneous (het-uh-ruh-JEE-nee-uhs)—made up of parts that are different.

homogeneous (hoh-muh-JEE-nee-uhs)—of uniform structure or composition throughout.

hypothesis (hye-PAH-thi-sis)—an unproven idea or theory based on known facts that leads to further study.

solute—a substance that is dissolved in another substance.

solvent—a substance that can make another substance dissolve.

soot—a black, powdery material formed from burning coal, wood, oil, or other fuel.

variety—a collection of different things or different types of one thing.

ONLINE RESOURCES

To learn more about mixtures and solutions, please visit **abdobooklinks.com** or scan this QR code. These links are routinely monitored and updated to provide the most current information available.

INDEX

alloys, 10

baking soda, 28, 29
brass, 10

carbon dioxide, 18
chemical reactions, 20
chemists, 24, 27
chromatography, 22, 24, 26
colloids, 14
concentration, 18
copper, 10
crystals, 28, 19

dissolving, 4, 6, 10, 14, 16, 18, 20
distillation, 22

evaporation, 28
experiments, 26, 27, 28, 29

gases, 4, 10, 14, 18, 22

heterogeneous, 6, 8
homogeneous, 6, 8, 10

liquids, 4, 10, 12, 22

metals, 10, 24

oil, 12

salt, 4, 10, 16, 18, 29
sand, 14, 22
saturation, 16, 18, 28
scientific method, 27
scientists, 18, 27
smoke, 14
solids, 4, 10, 22
solubility, 16
solutes, 10, 12, 14, 16, 18, 22, 29
solutions, 4, 10, 12, 14, 16, 18, 22, 28
solvents, 10, 12, 14, 16, 18
soot, 14
sugar, 6, 8, 20, 29
suspensions, 14, 22

temperature, 16, 18, 22

water, 4, 6, 8, 10, 12, 14, 16, 18, 20, 22, 26, 28

zinc, 10